W9-AET-872

Fact Finders®

WHAT WENT WRONG?

The 1918 Flu Pandemic

CORE EVENTS OF A WORLDWIDE OUTBREAK

by John Micklos Jr.

Consultant:
John M. Barry
Tulane University School of Public
Health and Tropical Medicine
New Orleans

CAPSTONE PRESS
a capstone imprint

Fact Finders Books are published by Capstone Press,
1710 Roe Crest Drive, North Mankato, Minnesota 56003
www.capstonepub.com

Library of Congress Cataloging-in-Publication Data
Micklos, John.
  The 1918 flu pandemic: core events of a worldwide outbreak / by John Micklos Jr.
    pages cm.—(Fact finders. What went wrong?)
  Includes bibliographical references and index.
  Summary: "Explains the 1918 Flu Pandemic, including its chronology, causes, and lasting effects"—
Provided by publisher.
  ISBN 978-1-4914-2045-4 (library binding)
  ISBN 978-1-4914-2220-5 (paperback)
  ISBN 978-1-4914-2235-9 (eBook PDF)
1. Influenza Epidemic, 1918–1919—Juvenile literature. 2. Influenza—History—20th century—
Juvenile literature. I. Title.
  RC150.4.M53 2015
  614.5'1809041—dc23   2014036875

Editorial Credits
Jenny Loomis, editor; Bobbie Nuytten, designer; Tracy Cummins, media researcher;
Charmaine Whitman, production specialist

Photo Credits
AP Images: National Museum of Health, 1, Cover bottom; CDC: Cynthia Goldsmith, 12, James
Gathany, 27; Corbis: Bettmann, 21, 22, GraphicaArtis, 24; Getty Images: AFP PHOTO/Philippe Lopez,
13 Left, AFP PHOTO/TIM SLOAN, 29, Hulton Archive/Paul Thompson, 18, MPI, 16, Popperfoto/
Paul Popper, 14; Library of Congress: 6, 9, 20; National Archives and Records Administration: 8,
Cover Top; Courtesy of the National Museum of Health and Medicine: Matthew Breitbart/AFIP
16635, 28; Newscom: akg-images, 11, Everett Collection, 5, 7, 19; Science Source: 13 Right, 26,
BSIP, 17; Shutterstock: djem, Design Element, Sergio77, Design Element; The Granger Collection: 25;
Wikimedia: The History of Medicine, 23.

Printed in Canada.
092014   008478FRS15

Table of Contents

Roscoe Vaughan was just 21 years old when he arrived at U.S. Army post Camp Jackson in South Carolina in September 1918. Like many young soldiers, he was preparing to go to Europe to fight in World War I (1914–1918). In the war, Great Britain, France, and the United States battled against Germany. In just over four years the war claimed 8.5 million lives.

Private Vaughan never got to fight the Germans. Instead a far deadlier enemy killed him. When he reached camp, thousands of sick soldiers were flooding the hospital. Nearly all had the influenza virus, which most people called the flu.

On September 19 Private Vaughan saw the camp doctor. Like many others Vaughan had a bad cough and a high fever. He ached all over. A week later he died, gasping for breath. An **autopsy** found that Vaughan's chest cavity was full of blood and other fluids. He had literally drowned.

FLU FACT

An estimated 40 to 50 million people worldwide died from influenza between 1918 and 1919. Some believe the number is closer to 100 million. In the United States, about 28 percent of the U.S. population got the flu in 1918 and 1919.

autopsy—examination of a corpse to determine cause of death

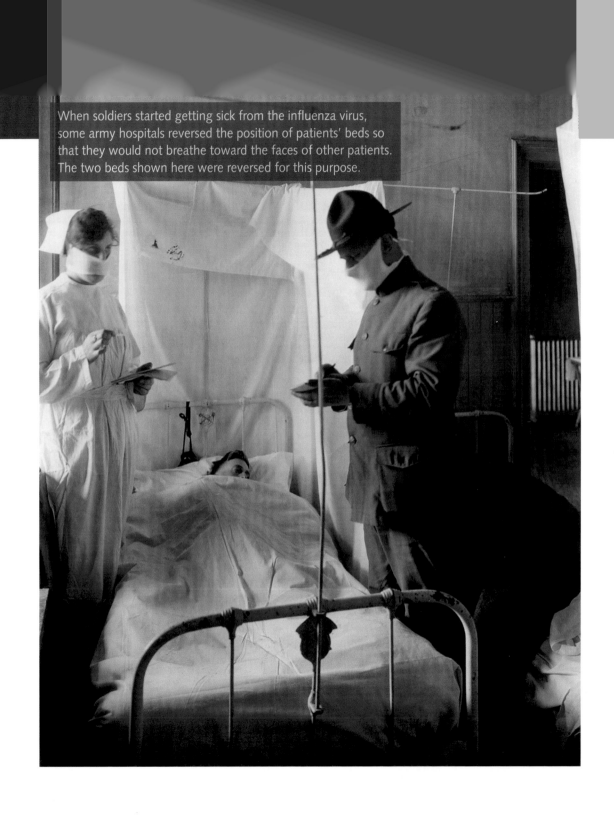

When soldiers started getting sick from the influenza virus, some army hospitals reversed the position of patients' beds so that they would not breathe toward the faces of other patients. The two beds shown here were reversed for this purpose.

"Three-Day Fever"

The camp doctor cut a small piece from Private Vaughan's lung. He packed the tissue sample in **formaldehyde** and candle wax and sent the sample to Washington, D.C. to be examined. But scientists at the time were unable to figure out what was causing the disease.

No one knows for certain where or when this flu **outbreak** first occurred. Evidence suggests three possibilities: Europe in 1915, China in 1917, and Haskell County, Kansas, in the United States in January 1918. One outbreak happened in March 1918 at the U.S. Army base in Fort Riley, Kansas. Within a month 1,100 soldiers became ill.

WHY WAS IT CALLED THE SPANISH FLU?

Bad news was considered harmful to the wartime effort. The press wasn't allowed to talk or write about the flu. Since Spain wasn't involved in World War I, its newspapers were the first to include news about the flu. This made people around the world mistakenly think that the virus started in Spain.

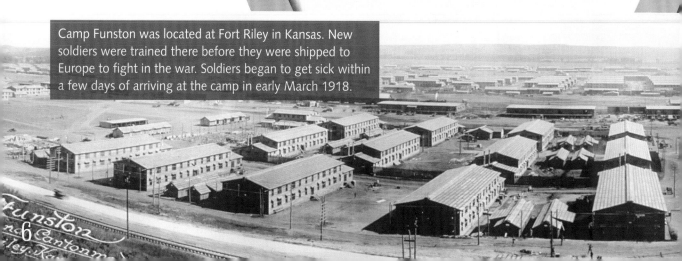

Camp Funston was located at Fort Riley in Kansas. New soldiers were trained there before they were shipped to Europe to fight in the war. Soldiers began to get sick within a few days of arriving at the camp in early March 1918.

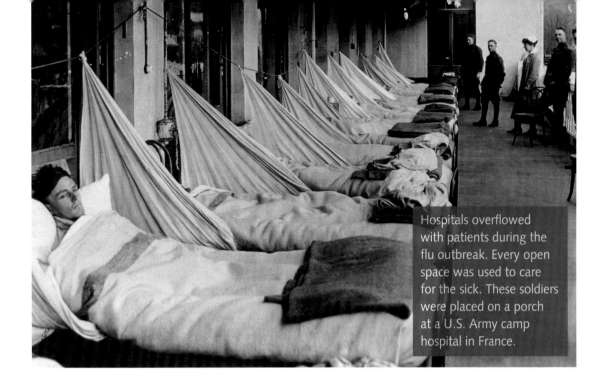

Hospitals overflowed with patients during the flu outbreak. Every open space was used to care for the sick. These soldiers were placed on a porch at a U.S. Army camp hospital in France.

Soon soldiers from Fort Riley shipped out to join the war effort in Europe. Some carried flu germs with them. By late spring the flu had spread to British, French, and German troops. Soldiers called the disease the "three-day fever." Most victims were very ill for three days and then began to feel better.

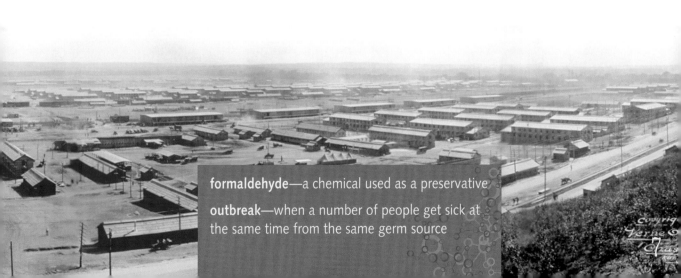

formaldehyde—a chemical used as a preservative

outbreak—when a number of people get sick at the same time from the same germ source

A Second Wave

The flu had become a **pandemic** by spring. People around the world were showing symptoms, although some places were hit hard while others were not affected at all. By the summer of 1918, the flu appeared to be going away. Then another wave struck. In late August sailors stationed in Boston showed flu symptoms. Soon **civilians** got sick too. Within weeks the flu spread throughout the United States.

This second wave of the flu proved far deadlier than the first. Places unaffected by the first wave were now being struck hard. The disease spread to millions of people throughout the world.

Despite the flu threat, many people were celebrating in the fall of 1918. Germany surrendered in November, and the terrible war had come to an end. But people were still not safe. A third wave of cases struck in early 1919.

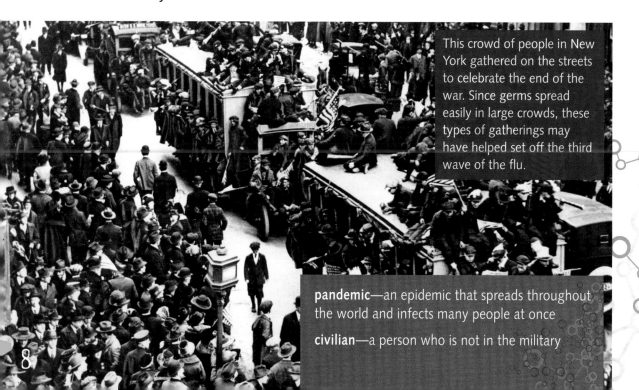

This crowd of people in New York gathered on the streets to celebrate the end of the war. Since germs spread easily in large crowds, these types of gatherings may have helped set off the third wave of the flu.

pandemic—an epidemic that spreads throughout the world and infects many people at once

civilian—a person who is not in the military

THE PRESIDENT GETS THE FLU

Even famous and powerful people got the flu. King Alfonso XIII of Spain and U.S. President Woodrow Wilson suffered through the flu. So did the emperor of Ethiopia. All three leaders survived.

President Wilson became sick in April 1919 while attending peace talks in Paris, France. His illness made it impossible for him to attend some of the meetings. He became violently ill so suddenly that at first doctors thought he had been poisoned.

Almost as suddenly as the flu had arrived, it disappeared. By the spring of 1919 fewer and fewer cases were reported. By summer no new cases were reported. But the disease left behind a trail of sadness and death. Nearly one in five people throughout the world had been infected. That figure was even higher in the United States, where more than one in every four people became ill.

In the United States an estimated 675,000 people died during the flu pandemic. Most scientists believe at least 40 million people died worldwide. Some think the figure is even higher.

At the time no one knew what started the flu outbreak or why it ended so suddenly. The disease remained a mystery for more than 80 years.

1918 Flu Pandemic Timeline

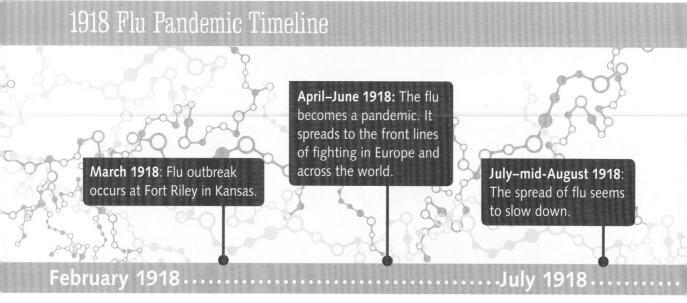

March 1918: Flu outbreak occurs at Fort Riley in Kansas.

April–June 1918: The flu becomes a pandemic. It spreads to the front lines of fighting in Europe and across the world.

July–mid-August 1918: The spread of flu seems to slow down.

February 1918 . . . . July 1918 . . . .

These American Red Cross (ARC) workers in St. Louis, Missouri, drove flu patients to hospitals. The ARC in St. Louis owned five ambulances and used them 24 hours a day during the second flu wave. The ambulances sometimes transported more than 100 patients in one day.

Late August–early December 1918: A second and deadlier wave of flu sweeps the world, killing millions.

Late December 1918: Another slowdown in new flu cases in some cities leads to hope that the pandemic is ending.

January–April 1919: The number of cases rises for a third time in the first months of the year. Then new cases level off and begin to decline.

June 1919: Except for a few cases, the pandemic ends, leaving an estimated 40 million people dead.

December 1918 .... June 1919

Scientists now know what causes influenza outbreaks. The flu is a virus that attacks the **respiratory system**. There are three main types of flu. Types B and C attack humans. Type A causes the most dangerous virus outbreaks and can attack humans, birds, pigs, horses, and other mammals. The 1918–1919 flu pandemic was a Type A virus.

The Type A virus can spread in different ways. The natural home for flu viruses is wild birds, which carry the virus. But it can sometimes spread to chickens that people raise on farms, and from there it can jump to pigs and other mammals.

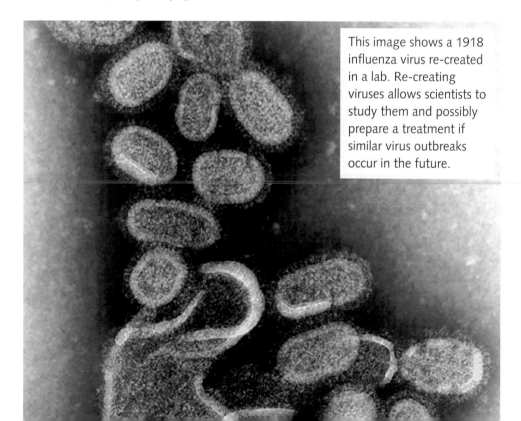

This image shows a 1918 influenza virus re-created in a lab. Re-creating viruses allows scientists to study them and possibly prepare a treatment if similar virus outbreaks occur in the future.

To help prevent another flu pandemic, chickens and pigs on farms are regularly checked for avian flu and swine flu. It is also recommended that the two types of animals are kept in separate areas on farms and not allowed contact with each other. This helps prevent any possible mixing of swine and avian viruses.

When pigs catch the avian (bird) flu virus, it can mix with their own swine (pig) flu virus. This creates a new virus form that can infect humans. People can also catch avian flu directly from chickens and ducks. Researchers believe that the 1918–1919 flu pandemic began in birds, then moved to some type of mammal before humans caught it.

Many **strains** of the flu just make people ill. Most victims recover after a few days. Normally very few people die.

respiratory system—the parts of the body that handle breathing and supply the blood with oxygen

strain—illnesses that share common symptoms but have characteristics that make them different

13

Spread by Soldiers

As soldiers moved throughout the world, so did the disease. First the Fort Riley soldiers carried the flu with them to Europe in the spring of 1918. While in Europe soldiers lived bunched together in **trenches** as the war raged around them. The close contact allowed the flu to quickly spread to British, French, and German soldiers.

Then in late August soldiers returned to the United States carrying a more deadly form of the disease. Many of these soldiers passed through the port city of Boston. The disease spread inland and then made its way west across the United States.

Thousands of miles across the Atlantic Ocean, two other major port cities, one in Africa and one in France, received sick soldiers at the same time as Boston. The virus again spread inland and beyond. Its devastation was felt worldwide.

Life in the trenches was difficult before the flu's arrival. Trenches were full of rats, flies, dead bodies, and thick, slimy mud. Once the flu started to spread quickly through the trenches, it only added to the soldiers' misery.

trench—a long, narrow ditch dug in the ground to serve as shelter from enemy fire or attack

Gasping for Breath

A normal flu causes aches and fever. People often vomit or have diarrhea but feel better after a few days. The flu of late 1918 and early 1919 had far deadlier symptoms. Victims gasped for breath as their lungs filled with fluid. Skin turned bluish-black from lack of oxygen. The infected coughed up blood, bled from their noses, and sometimes they even bled from their ears and eyes. As fevers soared to 106°F (41°C), victims became delirious. Many people died within a few days. Some died within hours.

A normal flu outbreak might kill one in a thousand victims. This flu killed more than one out of every 50 people who became ill. In some places the death rate was even higher. The flu nearly wiped out some villages in Alaska and Africa. Most flu epidemics strike hardest among very young and very old people. This flu targeted healthy young adults, killing many of them.

People had never dealt with such a disease. Doctors had no idea why the virus was so deadly. No one knew how to avoid it.

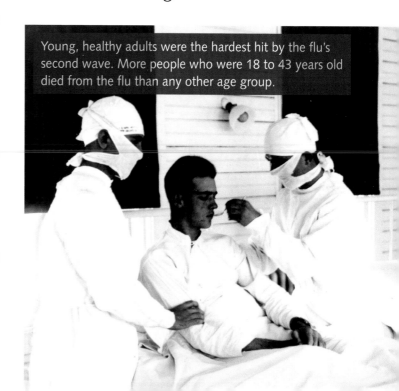

Young, healthy adults were the hardest hit by the flu's second wave. More people who were 18 to 43 years old died from the flu than any other age group.

16

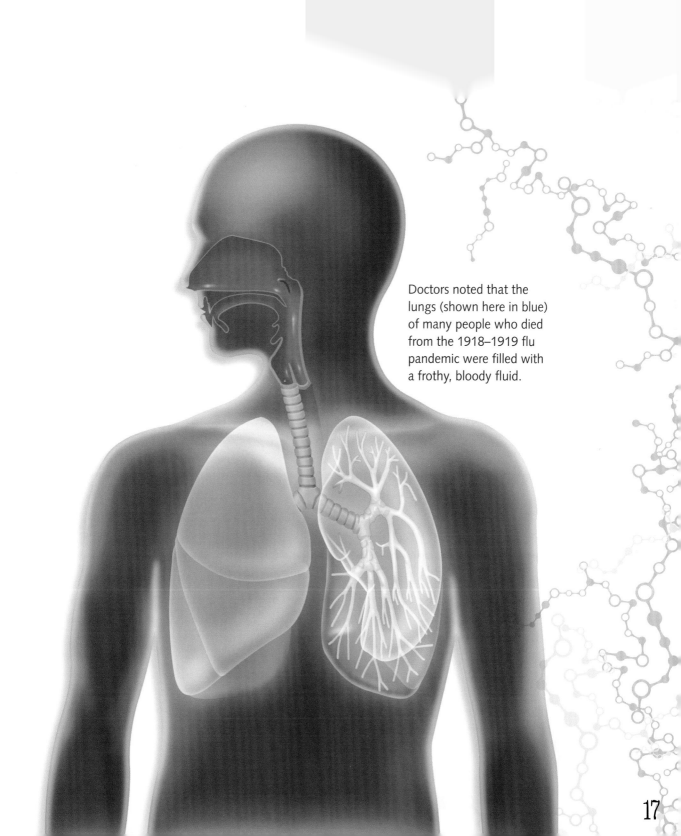

Doctors noted that the lungs (shown here in blue) of many people who died from the 1918–1919 flu pandemic were filled with a frothy, bloody fluid.

CHAPTER 3

No Cause, No Cure

The first wave of the flu pandemic affected armies on both sides of the war. The disease quickly spread through damp trenches and crowded ships. The U.S. Navy reported that nearly half of its sailors got the flu in 1918. More than one in three U.S. Army soldiers battled the disease.

Other armies faced the same problems. British warships could not get out to sea for weeks because so many sailors were sick. A German army weakened by flu lost an important battle in July. Still, most who grew sick with the disease recovered in a few days.

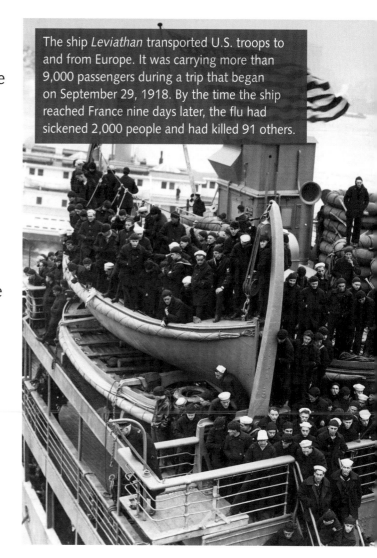

The ship *Leviathan* transported U.S. troops to and from Europe. It was carrying more than 9,000 passengers during a trip that began on September 29, 1918. By the time the ship reached France nine days later, the flu had sickened 2,000 people and had killed 91 others.

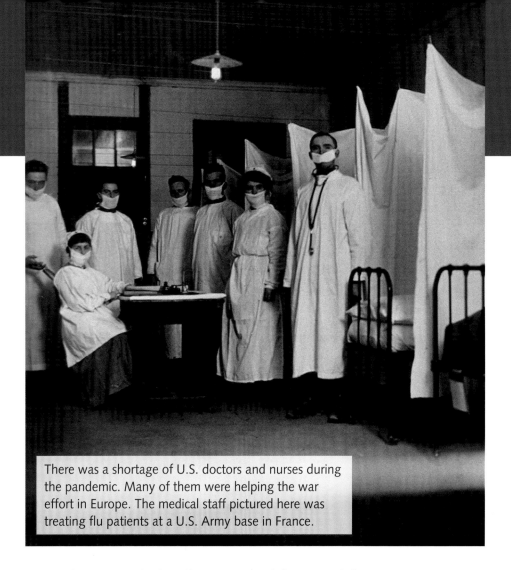

There was a shortage of U.S. doctors and nurses during the pandemic. Many of them were helping the war effort in Europe. The medical staff pictured here was treating flu patients at a U.S. Army base in France.

The second, deadlier wave of flu posed far greater problems. As the disease spread, doctors' offices and hospitals were overwhelmed. Some doctors and nurses caught the disease too. This left even fewer people to treat the sick. As the death toll rose, **morgues** overflowed. In some towns public funerals were banned for fear the disease would spread.

morgue—a place where dead bodies are kept until burial

In Philadelphia thousands of people grew ill in September and October of 1918. City officials decided to close schools, churches, and other places where people gathered. They hoped the closings would stop the disease from spreading. It didn't stop. Within a month nearly 11,000 people in Philadelphia died from the flu.

Many cities looked like ghost towns. Stores closed because so many workers were sick. There were hardly any customers anyway. People were afraid to go out in public. They even feared inviting friends and relatives into their homes.

Pharmacists worked long hours during the flu pandemic to keep up with the demand for medicine.

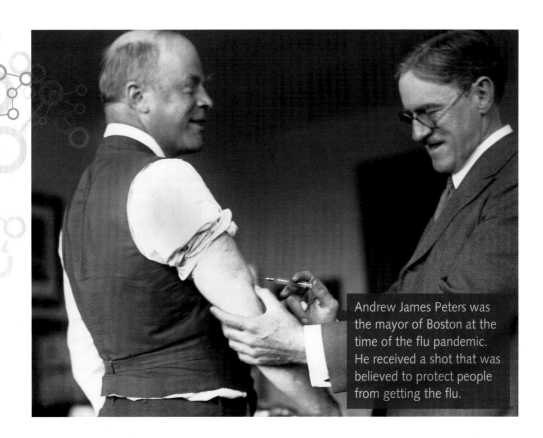

Andrew James Peters was the mayor of Boston at the time of the flu pandemic. He received a shot that was believed to protect people from getting the flu.

Because doctors and scientists didn't fully understand influenza, they couldn't stop it. The disease had no cure. No one knew about the virus that caused it. Still, scientists tried to create a **vaccine**. In San Francisco, 20,000 people received flu shots. Many of them got sick anyway.

Some people tried homemade cures. They ate chicken soup. They wore **camphor** balls. They even took doses of kerosene. Nothing seemed to work.

vaccine—a medicine that prevents a disease

camphor—a gummy, fragrant substance found in the wood and bark of a camphor tree

The type of masks used during the flu pandemic offered limited protection against the virus.

Doctors and public health officials knew they couldn't cure the flu. All they could do was try to prevent it from spreading. Sick people were **quarantined** in their homes. In some cities even healthy people had to wear masks in public. Health officials hoped this would prevent the spread of flu germs.

In the end the only real solution was time. By June 1919 the disease had run its course. The long months of flu terror ended as suddenly as they began.

As a result of the flu pandemic, many positive changes were made. Doctors encouraged people to be more careful about sneezing, coughing, and spitting in public places. Meanwhile, scientists kept working to learn more about the virus that caused the flu.

By the early 1940s, a flu vaccine was developed for U.S. soldiers who were fighting in World War II (1939–1945). Soon after the war, civilians could get it too. Today many people get a flu shot each year. The vaccine protects against the most common strains of flu.

A PLACE OF SAFETY

Australia felt the effects of flu far less than most places. What kept them safe? For months Australia quarantined all arriving ships. Keeping newcomers separated prevented sick people from entering the country. The flu did not slip into Australia until December 1918.

Public places, such as buses and theaters, were full of posters like this during the flu pandemic. The purpose for the posters was to teach people how to help prevent the flu from spreading.

PREVENT DISEASE

CARELESS SPITTING, COUGHING, SNEEZING, SPREAD INFLUENZA and TUBERCULOSIS

RENSSELAER COUNTY TUBERCULOSIS ASSOCIATION, TROY, N.Y.

quarantine—to keep a person away from others to stop a disease from spreading

23

The flu pandemic of 1918 ranks among the deadliest events of all time. It certainly killed the most people in the shortest period of time. It can be compared to other killer diseases that have swept the world. These diseases include smallpox, the plague, cholera, and AIDS.

Smallpox has been around for centuries. The disease is similar to chicken pox but much more serious. About one in three people who got the disease died. Smallpox played a major role in the Spanish conquests of the Incas and Aztecs. The native population had no **immunity** against this deadly disease that the Spanish brought from Europe. Smallpox weakened the Inca and Aztec populations and allowed small Spanish armies to conquer them.

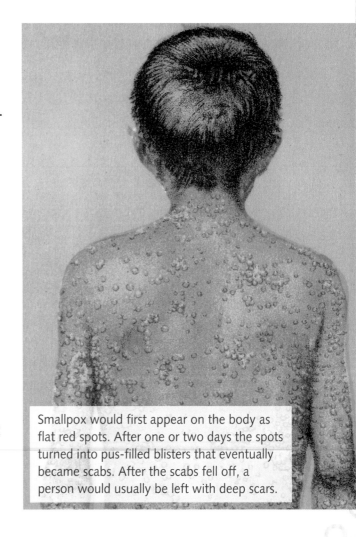

Smallpox would first appear on the body as flat red spots. After one or two days the spots turned into pus-filled blisters that eventually became scabs. After the scabs fell off, a person would usually be left with deep scars.

immunity—the ability of the body to resist a poison or disease

This wood engraving shows poor New York City residents receiving a vaccine for smallpox inside a police station in 1872.

Some scientists believe smallpox killed as many as 300 million people in the 1900s alone. The disease has now been eliminated with the help of vaccines. There have been no cases of smallpox since 1977.

SHORTENED LIFESPANS

The average life expectancy in the United States in 1917 and 1919 was 51 years. In 1918 the average life expectancy was only 39 years. What caused that drastic difference? More than half a million people in the United States died from the flu in 1918. Many of them were in their 20s and 30s. This caused the average life expectancy for that year to be much lower than usual.

The Black Plague swept Europe in the 1300s. It killed 30 to 60 percent of Europe's entire population. One strain, known as the bubonic plague, caused swelling in the neck, armpits, and groin. The areas oozed pus and blood. People were afraid to get near victims for fear of catching the disease. Another strain attacked the lungs and killed nearly all its victims.

Acquired Immune Deficiency Syndrome (AIDS) has killed more than 24 million people since it was first recognized in 1981. Scientists have developed drugs to help treat the symptoms of AIDS, but they continue to search for a cure. Cholera, malaria, and typhus have also claimed millions of lives over the years.

During the Black Plague drivers of "death carts" would travel up and down streets calling, "Bring out your dead!" Because bodies piled up too quickly for proper burial, they were thrown onto the carts and then dumped into pits. The cart drivers smoked pipes to cover the odor of decaying bodies. The drivers also thought tobacco smoke protected them from the plague.

Unlike the flu pandemic, most of these other diseases killed their victims over decades. The flu pandemic claimed nearly all of its victims within a single year. Historian Alfred Crosby called 1918 the deadliest year in human history.

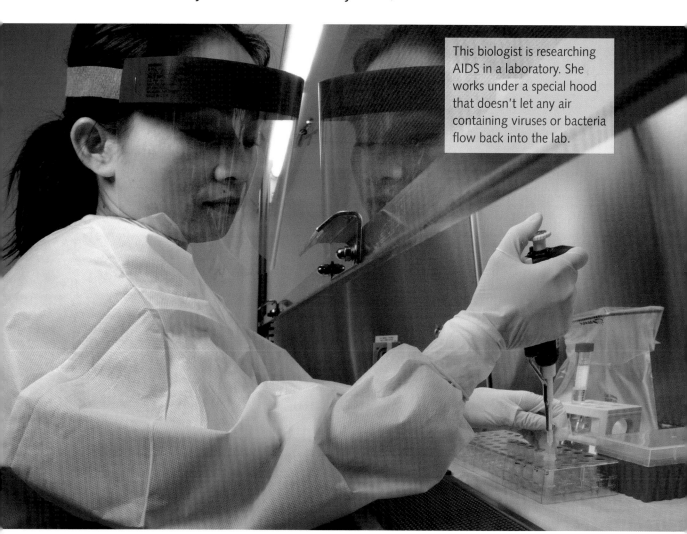

This biologist is researching AIDS in a laboratory. She works under a special hood that doesn't let any air containing viruses or bacteria flow back into the lab.

Flu outbreaks that have occurred in recent history have been mild in comparison to the deadly 1918 pandemic. These include the swine flu in 1976, the avian flu that first occurred in Hong Kong in 1997, and the H1N1 swine flu of 2009. The H1N1 flu affected about 50 million Americans or one in every six people. About 11,000 people died. That strain was mild, and treatment options were far better than they were in 1918.

Understanding the Virus

In the 1990s researchers tried to learn more about the 1918 flu virus. They examined tissue from U.S. soldiers who had died, including

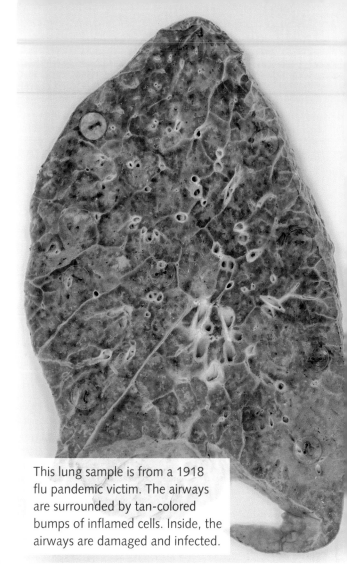

This lung sample is from a 1918 flu pandemic victim. The airways are surrounded by tan-colored bumps of inflamed cells. Inside, the airways are damaged and infected.

the tissue sample from Private Roscoe Vaughan. Researchers analyzed the virus. They found that the 1918 virus could attach to cells in both the upper respiratory system, including the nose and throat, and in the lungs of the lower respiratory system. The typical flu virus can only attach itself to the upper respiratory system.

This 5-year-old boy is getting the H1N1 flu nasal mist. Recent studies suggest that the flu mist is more effective for children between the ages of 2 through 8 than the flu shot.

People wonder what the next pandemic might be. Will it be a vaccine-resistant strain of flu that moves from birds or pigs to people? Will it be some new form of plague? This sounds like the plot from a science fiction movie, but history has shown that anything is possible.

FLU FACT

When the 1997 outbreak of avian flu occurred in Hong Kong, officials killed more than 1 million chickens to prevent the disease from spreading.

Glossary

autopsy (AW-top-see)—an examination of a corpse to determine the cause of death

camphor (KAM-fuhr)—a gummy, fragrant substance found in the wood and bark of a camphor tree

civilian (si-VIL-yuhn)—a person who is not in the military

formaldehyde (for-MEL-duh-hyd)—a chemical used as a preservative

immunity (i-MYOON-uh-tee)—the ability of the body to resist a poison or disease

morgue (MORG)—a place where dead bodies are kept until burial

outbreak (OWT-brayk)—when a number of people get sick at the same time from the same germ source

pandemic (pan-DEM-ik)—an epidemic that spreads throughout the world and infects many people at once

quarantine (KWOR-uhn-teen)—to keep a person away from others to stop a disease from spreading

respiratory system (RESS-pi-ruh-taw-ree SIS-tum)—the parts of the body that handle breathing and supply the blood with oxygen

strain (STRAYN)—illnesses that share common symptoms but have characteristics that make them different

trench (TRENCH)—a long, narrow ditch dug in the ground to serve as shelter from enemy fire or attack

vaccine (vak-SEEN)—a medicine that prevents a disease

Internet Sites

FactHound offers a safe, fun way to find Internet sites related to this book. All of the sites on FactHound have been researched by our staff.

Here's all you do:

Visit *www.facthound.com*

Type in this code: 9781491420454

Check out projects, games and lots more at
www.capstonekids.com

Critical Thinking Using the Common Core

1. Look at the timeline on pages 10–11. How much time passed between the slowdown of the flu's first wave and the beginning of the second wave? How much time passed between the slowdown of the second wave and the beginning of the third wave? What does this say about the strength of this virus? (Craft and Structure)

2. Describe how soldiers' movements between different parts of the world during World War I contributed to the flu pandemic. (Key Idea and Details)

3. How well do you think the United States and other countries are prepared for another flu pandemic? Support your answer with facts from the text as well as from research from print and online sources. (Integration of Knowledge and Ideas)

Read More

Koontz, Robin Michal. *The Science of a Pandemic*. Disaster Science. Ann Arbor, Mich.: Cherry Lake Publishing, 2014.

Marciniak, Kristin. *The Flu Pandemic of 1918*. History's Greatest Disasters. Minneapolis: ABDO, 2013.

Rudolph, Jessica. *The Flu of 1918: Millions Dead Worldwide!* Nightmare Plagues. New York: Bearport Publishing, 2011.

Index